The Prestige

Barton

John Banks
Photography by G H F Atkins

Cover: One of the pleasures of motoring on the Continent is happening across vehicles from favourite British fleets. Here, in France in 1966, two Barton coaches engaged on tours were spotted. Number **1073** (**FVO 73D**), a brand new Plaxton-bodied Bedford VAM 45-seater, was going to Germany and Austria, and 1959 Duple-bodied AEC Reliance No. **933** (**239 CNN**) was bound for the Italian Lakes.

Rear cover: A pleasant scene at Stamford bus station on 8th August 1969. Present were Barton Nos **1019** (**BVO 19C**) and **870** (**870 HAL**). Both Bedford SBs - an SB5 and an SB1 - they were bodied by Harrington and Plaxton respectively. *(John Banks)* In the inset is the familiar logo, widely used after the acquisition of Robin Hood (Coaches) Ltd in October 1961.

Inside Rear cover: On 8th August 1969 Barton/Hall Brothers Nos **H9** (**JFT 258**) and **H29** (**CFT 203D**), respectively a Plaxton-bodied Bedford SB5 and a Duple Northern-bodied Ford R192, and **H25** (**DCU 146D**), a Plaxton-bodied AEC Reliance, were hastening south in convoy on the A1 in West Yorkshire. *(Both: John Banks)*

Title page: One of the most striking features of the Barton fleet was the number of in-house-built buses and coaches it contained over the years. Early experiments abounded but the production in the early postwar period of the BTS1 vehicles was unparalleled for an independent operator, even one as big as Barton. Number **631** (**LNN 802**) was the first of the BTS1s. Its chassis was constructed from two prewar Leyland double-deckers: the front half from ex-Burnley Colne & Nelson No. 60, a TD3c, and the rear half from ex-Plymouth TD4c No. 139. The striking "Road Master" body was by Beccols, to dual-purpose 43-seat specification. The vehicle entered service in August 1950 and was photographed in that same month at Huntingdon Street bus station, Nottingham. It was withdrawn in 1960.

Opposite page: Late afternoon long shadows at Kegworth in August 1934 and the photographer includes his shadow self-portrait in his picture of No. **150** (**VO 7401**) passing by on service 10 to Nottingham. The vehicle was a Leyland-bodied Leyland Lion LT5, which had been new in 1932.

Below: Barton Leyland Lions and a Trent SOS at Huntingdon Street in January 1936. Number **207** (**BAL 407**), a 1935 Lion LT7 with Duple coachwork is the centre vehicle of the trio.

Although he had seen and noted Barton vehicles around in the fifties, the writer was seriously introduced to the full magnificence of the Barton fleet on a visit to its headquarters at Chilwell in the early 1960s. Armed with 19 shots left in his camera and a spare 36-exposure film in his pocket he was, after a quarter of an hour, canvassing fellow members of the party to see whether they could sell him some spare films - not film in the singular, mind you, but films, and the more the better. Barton was that sort of fleet. It might be trite to say that no two of its vehicles were alike, and not strictly accurate, but that is how it felt and there were more variations to photograph than in any other fleet.

Having comprised 100 vehicles in the late 1920s, by the time the writer was becoming absorbed with it the fleet was usually at a strength of just under 300 (in 1953 it was 290

and a consistent 251 in 1982), though it peaked at 336 plus 35 Hall Brothers vehicles in 1967. Vehicle numbering was a remarkably simple and effective straight numerical system starting at 1 and reaching 500 in 1947; the magic 1000 came in 1964 and in 1976 the numbers dropped the "1" and continued as three-figure numbers, 1464 being the last four-figure number and 465 the first of the revised series; it was still a strict incremental series and had reached 645 by 1989 when Barton sold out.

So much for the writer: the photographer, Geoffrey Atkins, started taking transport pictures in 1927 and was soon attracted to Barton. Resources were limited at first - Geoffrey was then 15 and restricted to a simple vest pocket Kodak bought by his parents as a reward for doing well at school - and money for films and travelling around in pursuit of his hobby was scarce. By the late 1930s, however, spurred on by the magnificent series of Leyland Lion coaches put into service by Barton in that decade, he was taking more and more photographs in an endeavour to record all the complexities of the rapidly evolving Barton fleet.

Barton was ever in the forefront of the movement to achieve the highest seating capacity possible within the law and - in desperation at the infuriating slowness of officialdom to reorganise archaic regulations - sometimes outside it. The founder of the Company, Thomas Henry Barton, bought his

*Barton often produced novelty vehicles aimed at publicity and marketing. **RR 6076** was a Lea Francis private car chassis rebodied as a publicity van by Duple in 1935. (Senior Transport Archive)*

(John Banks Collection)

The
BARTON
*Motor Omnibus &
Touring Services*

first vehicle in 1897 and in 1908 the Barton operation that was to survive and prosper began with a Durham-Churchill *char-à-bancs* operating a service between Long Eaton and Nottingham.

Seldom satisfied with proprietary manufacturers' efforts, Barton modified and rebuilt a wide variety of machines, usually in order to increase their seating capacity. Notable in this respect was a pair of 1923 solid-tyred Daimlers that were respectively lengthened to 34ft 2ins and 36½ feet to seat 60 and 66 - figures unheard of in those days. Even more noteworthy was a series of "Barton Gilders", where four-wheeled chassis were lengthened and fitted with a second rear axle. Perhaps the most remarkable vehicle was a low-loading, hoop-framed machine with two engines, although it never ran in service.

Through the 1920s the fleet relied in the main on Daimler Y types and Lancias, although AEC, Morris and Ford were represented, as were such

Upper: *Not the Barton family's first venture into road transport, but generally regarded as the first true Barton Transport vehicle, Durham Churchill char-à-bancs, registration number **W 963**, is seen at Long Eaton in 1908. (Photographer unknown)*

Lower: *In 1952 a replica of the body that had been carried by the Durham Churchill was constructed and mounted on a solid-tyred Daimler chassis. It was photographed outside the Barton office in Huntingdon Street, Nottingham, in June 1953.*

as Chevrolet and Gilford. Around 1930 Barton's own productions were playing an increasing part but as the new decade progressed, although much variety remained - AEC, Reo, Maudslay, Commer, Minerva, TSM, Dennis, Crossley, Bedford, etc. - often acquired second-hand from other operators, the love affair between Barton and Leyland Motors was beginning. The decade saw a splendid fleet of four-cylinder Leyland Lions, augmented by a small number of six-cylinder Tigers, placed into service. Before the war the majority of vehicles were single-deckers: there had been early, solid-tyred double-deckers, a few rather

bizarre open-top Gilfords in the late 1920s, and a handful of conventional Leyland Titans in the thirties as well as a pair of acquired AEC Regents, but it was the war that brought about the building up of a substantial fleet of double-deckers. Many second-hand Leyland Titans were bought and there was an allocation of utility AEC Regents and Guy Arabs from the Ministry of War Transport.

In the early postwar period, Leyland was again the favoured chassis supplier, and large numbers of PS1/1 Tigers and PD1 Titan double-deckers were purchased, augmented by some Bedford OB coaches and an amazing - no other

*To describe this pair of pictures as "A Half-Century of DIY" might be a little prosaic, having regard to the engineering skills required to complete such projects, but - in that the chassis were not off-the-shelf offerings from proprietary manufacturers - it would be accurate. In the upper picture, we see a lengthened 1923 Daimler, No. **10 (NN 3561)**, which was 36½ft long and had 66 seats. It ran, despite the disapproval of the authorities, until 1929. Forty-six years later Barton were still producing much-modified vehicles, as in the case of No. **1135 (YRR 513H)**, a Barton BTS2 chassis that was made up from a rebuilt and modified AEC Reliance chassis - No. 927 (SNN 399) - to which was fitted a new Plaxton 45-seat coach body. There were ten such rebuilds in 1969, all withdrawn in 1974. The picture was taken in Huntingdon Street in 1970. (Upper picture: Photographer unknown)*

word for it - collection of second-hand vehicles, either acquired through takeovers of other operators or bought through dealers.

Perhaps the most remarkable achievement among many were the in-house building programmes that produced the BTS1, BTD2 and BTS2 Barton-built vehicles, based on used Leyland (BTS1 and BTD2) and AEC (BTS2) chassis. For the former, Barton proved itself not only an expert engineering organisation but also a competent coachbuilder, producing some of the most visually striking designs to be seen on Britain's roads in the nineteen-fifties.

As the decades passed there was no let up in the variety to be seen in the Barton single-deck fleet. All types of vehicles, from the four corners almost of the British Isles, with seating capacities from eleven to fifty-seven, were represented and very few of the major coachbuilders had not at least one of their products running in Barton colours.

Throughout the nineteen-sixties it seemed as though the status quo - batches of new vehicles augmented by Barton rebuilds or second-hand acquisitions - would go on for ever. It was not to be so. Barton did not, of course, run its fleet for the benefit of enthusiasts, and there was some dismay when it was learned that there was to be a restructuring and that finance was being sought for the fleet to be entirely replaced with Bedford YRQ and YRT models and Leyland Leopards, and that there were to be no double-deckers in future plans. A flash of the old entrepreneurial spirit lingered into the late 1960s, when the BTS2s were constructed from older AEC Reliance chassis, although all were conventionally bodied by Plaxton.

From the large collection of photographs available, most Barton types running from the thirties right up to and into that modern fleet of the seventies and eighties can be illustrated. After much thought, it has been decided the best way to present such a wealth of illustrations is to cover the single-deckers in this first part and to devote a second volume to the double-deckers.

As has been stated in earlier volumes featuring the work of Geoffrey Atkins, his first love is the art of the coachbuilder and his photography was mainly undertaken to reflect that. To some extent locations and even vehicle identities were secondary.

Acknowledgements

As the list of titles in the *Prestige Series* and its kindred *Super Prestige* and *Colour Prestige* books grows longer, the writer is more than ever aware of the debt he owes to his friend Ron Maybray, who has once again been of otherwise unobtainable help in the provision of early vehicle information. The PSV Circle's publication PE8, dealing with Barton from 1960 to 1985 has been invaluable. Alan Oxley has vetted the text to its immense advantage and David and Mary Shaw have read and checked the proofs.

All photographs are from the John Banks Collection and were taken, unless stated otherwise in the captions, by Geoffrey Atkins.

The usual *caveat* is given: this book is neither a definitive history of Barton nor a fleet list. For that, the series of books on Barton by Alan Oxley, now running to three volumes - the first published by Venture's predecessor, the Transport Publishing Company, and the rest by Robin Hood Publishing - are thoroughly recommended.

John Banks
Romiley, Cheshire
August 2003

*Buses with three axles were in vogue in the late 1920s and again in the 1960s. The upper view is of a Barton-modified six-wheeled Lancia No. **45 (RR 2074)**. Whereas in those years three axles were needed for longer vehicles so that legal axle loadings were not exceeded, when the Bedford VAL came out its maximum dimensions were the same as those of two-axle vehicles. The twin axles with their small wheels were at the front instead of the rear; advantages were claimed for the layout and the type was popular for some years. Barton's No. **970 (414 SRR)** (lower) was a 1963 example with Plaxton 52-seat coachwork that lasted in the fleet until 1972. (Upper picture: Photographer unknown)*

Much of Barton's success was founded on its loyal and enthusiastic platform staff. The two gentlemen in the picture above were in charge of 1936 Leyland Tiger No. **294 (CVO 10)** at Lutterworth on the final day of a six-day Road Cruise to Devon and Cornwall on 21st May 1937. In the view below the same vehicle, with its passengers, was at Land's End. With a tours and excursions route-mileage of many thousands, Barton vehicles were likely to turn up anywhere in Great Britain as well as venturing on to the Continent. *(See also page 22.)*

The Barton single-deck fleet - A chronological survey

Above: The replica vehicle on the Daimler chassis, **W 963,** was no mascot, but rather a fully working vehicle that on this occasion had ventured as far as London to take part in a parade of vintage vehicles. The location was Piccadilly and the date September 1954. The vehicle was being driven by Barton's Managing Director, Mr T A Barton, and the occasion was a part of the silver jubilee celebrations of The Omnibus Society.

Below: Some thought went into whether or not to include this picture. A very early prentice job from the great Geoffrey Atkins, it was successful enough to reveal the fleet number **97** and the destination board "Nottingham & Skegness". The vehicle was registered **RR 9323** and was a Lancia Pentaiota of 1928. The canvas-roofed coachwork was to two-door 26-seat specification by Strachan & Brown and by the time of this picture a Barton radiator had been fitted.

Above: Number **98** (**RR 9501**) was a Commer 32-seater with bodywork by Challands Ross, new on 30th June 1928. The seating was described as dual-purpose, fitting the vehicle for use as either service bus or coach. In this picture it was brand new and it went into service in the Barton fleet on 21st July 1928 on the Nottingham to Leicester route. *(Challands Ross)*

Below: The same vehicle seen at a later date after Barton had altered the livery, suppressing the cream roof and cab front. It was at Huntingdon Street circa 1932 waiting to depart for Long Eaton.

Above: Number **132** (**VO 4296**) had chassis and body built by Barton as a rear-entrance 32-seat oil-engined bus. The power unit was a Gardner five-cylinder, making this probably the first five-cylinder Gardner-powered bus anywhere. It was photographed in Lower Parliament Street, Nottingham, in April 1932.

Below: Barton chassis No. **139** (**VO 5439**) was also oil-engined, and proudly said so on the waistrail: "No Petrol - Barton British Fuel Oil Bus - No Danger". The engine was a Blackstone, fitted when the vehicle was new in March 1931; it was later replaced by a Gilford 6-cylinder petrol Lycoming unit. The body was modified from Lancia-Barton No. 6, which had been normal control. The vehicle was running on trade plates **034 AL**, and was in South Sherwood Street, Nottingham.

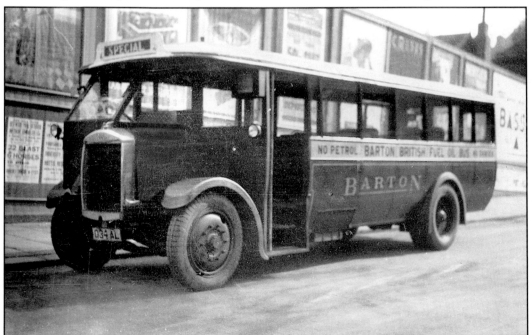

Above: In October 1933 the fleet of Ward's Bus Service Ltd, of Calverton, was acquired. Included among three vehicles added to the Barton fleet was No. **173** (**VO 3329**), an EMCO-bodied 26-seat Reo Pullman, which had been new in 1930. EMCO stood for Economy Manufacturing Company. The vehicle was photographed at Long Eaton in September 1934.

Below: Six months or so later, in May 1934, two vehicles came into the fleet from S Pounder, of Ilkeston, one of which was a rare Minerva Auto Traction, No. **177** (**TO 8801**), a 1928 Wilton-bodied 26-seater. Minerva Motors SA, of Antwerp, Belgium, who built vehicles from 1913 to 1957, acquired Auto Traction in 1925.

In the meantime Barton had been busy discovering Leyland (or *vice versa*) and in 1931 the first of a long series of Lion LT models was taken into stock. Numbers **142/3 (VO 6036/7)**, with Leyland 35-seat front-entrance bus bodies were LT2 models. In the first of two Huntingdon Street scenes, No. 142 is seen in one of Geoffrey Atkins's fine night shots in January 1936, and No. 143 *(below)* was in much the same place in July 1934. They were respectively on services to Melton Mowbray and Loughborough, both advertised by means of roofboards as the "most frequent service".

Above: The Leyland Lion LT5 model was the choice for 1933/4 when twelve were delivered. The bodies were to 35-seat design built by Leyland. Number **160 (VO 8411)** was on the Nottingham to Keyworth service at Huntingdon Street in August 1934.

Below: A similar vehicle was No. **168 (VO 9468)**. In October 1936 it was in Kent Street, Nottingham, apparently on tour duty.

Above: Two similar Lion LT5 chassis were fitted with 32-seat coach bodies by Duple for express work. The coachwork incorporated a luggage rack, which bore the legend "Barton Express". In June 1933 the first of them, No. **170** (**VO 9470**), was photographed at Roman Bank/Burgh Road, Skegness on the return journey to Nottingham.

Below: In a slightly later - August 1933 - picture, No. **170** had received minor changes to its livery in that the mudguards had been painted red instead of cream. This picture was taken at Huntingdon Street. The destination blind was set to "Private".

Above: Perhaps an unusual move, given the leaning towards Leyland Motors as main supplier of chassis to Barton, was the purchase in 1934 of No. **192** (**ARR 992**), an AEC Regal with Duple 32-seat coachwork. It may not have been well liked, for it was withdrawn in 1938, subsequently running for a variety of owners for another 22 years.

Below: Contemporary with the AEC was a pair of Leyland LT5A Lions, also with Duple 32-seat coachwork, which differed in many details from that on the AEC. Number **178** (**ARR 178**) was brand new when photographed at Sandiacre in May 1934. This vehicle and its twin No. 179 were sold in 1938: again, suspiciously early.

Above: Taken at around the same time, but at Huntingdon Street, Nottingham, another view of No. **178** displays the classic lines of the Duple coachwork.

Below: Also in 1934 came twelve LT5A Lions bodied by Brush as 39-seat dual-purpose vehicles. Representing the batch, at Huntingdon Street in 1934, was No. **189** (**ARR 189**). The Brush coachwork seems to have been heavily influenced by the contemporary Leyland design. In a further variation on a theme, there were two further LT5As in 1934, fitted with Willowbrook 39-seat dual-purpose coachwork.

Upper: In 1935 the Lion models purchased were the latest LT7 version. Twenty joined the fleet, all with Duple coachwork, some as 32-seat coaches and some as dual-purpose 39-seaters. One of the latter was No. **195** (**BAL 395**), seen on layover at Long Eaton on a short working of the Nottingham to Derby service in May 1935.

Centre: Nineteen-thirty-five saw the arrival of Barton's first Leyland Tiger: a TS6, again with Duple 32-seat coachwork. Number **210** (**BAL 410**) was brand new when this portrait was taken in April 1935.

Below: Number **210** again, in idyllic rural surroundings near Keyworth in May 1936. The vehicle was sold in November 1938.

Above: Nineteen-thirty-five was a good year for Barton in respect of the acquisition of other operators, among them H Squires, of Ruddington, taken over in the November. Five vehicles were acquired - two GMCs, two Crossleys and a Leyland Lion LT5A. One of the GMCs was **VO 4408**, new in 1930 and seen here at Ruddington before it passed to Barton, in whose fleet it became No. 246. It was withdrawn in 1936.

Below: In the same month another operator of the Ruddington service, E W Campion and Sons, of Nottingham, was taken over. Again, five vehicles passed to Barton - two AEC Regents and three Commers. The newest Commer was 1932 NF6 model **TV 5630**, which became Barton 251. It was photographed at Ruddington in October 1933.

Above: The flood of new Leyland LT7 Lions with Duple coachwork continued in 1936, and there were also two TS7 Tigers and ten Leyland Cubs, the latter bodied by Brush. Number **274** (**CNN 866**) was one of the Lions. A 39-seat dual-purpose vehicle, it was very recently into service in this Huntingdon Street view.

Below: Number **289** (**CRR 824**), another LT7 photographed at Huntingdon Street, had been painted in a special livery for the Coronation of King George VI. The picture dates from August 1937.

Upper: The 1936 Leyland Cubs were Brush-bodied 20-seat coaches based on the KPZ2 chassis. Seldom seen in photographs is that part of the streamlined beading and livery at the rear so well shown in this coachbuilder's picture of brand new No. **285** (**CRR 820**). *(Brush)*

Centre: Most of the Cubs lasted into the postwar period: in this Huntingdon Street picture taken soon after the end of the war, No. **283** (**CRR 818**) was standing in the street outside the bus station.

Lower: Number **270** (**BVO 470**) was the first of the pair of 1936 Leyland TS7 Tigers. The coachwork was by Duple and the vehicles were 32-seaters. The photograph dates from October 1937, again at Huntingdon Street. Number 270 went to the military in 1939 and was lost at Dunkirk by being driven into the sea.

For 1937 the new vehicle programme was an all-Leyland/Duple affair: TS7 Tigers with 32-seat coach bodies; LT7 Lions as 32-seat coaches and dual-purpose 39-seaters; and KPZ2 Cub 20-seaters. Number **294** (**CVO 10**), one of the TS7s, was the first of the intake, and was delivered late in 1936. This vehicle was used on Barton's Road Cruise No. 4 to Devon and Cornwall on the 1937 Whit Sunday (16th May) departure from Nottingham. Geoffrey Atkins was on board for this six-day holiday and two of the many pictures he took record No. 294 at Lyme Regis *(above)* and negotiating a typically narrow Cornish street *(below)*. The livery is again the special Coronation version, with prominent crest on the radiator. *(See also page 8.)*

Above: One of the Duple-bodied Leyland Lion LT7s at Wilford Lane, Nottingham, in January 1940. Heavy snow falls followed by a rapid thaw were making the going difficult. This was wartime, and the headlamps are masked and front wingtips painted white: the one to reduce visibility for enemy bomber crews and the other to increase it for pedestrians stumbling around in the blackout.

Below: A similar vehicle, this one identifiable as 1935's No. **214** (**BRR 297**), at around the same time - perhaps a few days earlier, before the thaw set in - makes its way gently through thick snow. The location was Mansfield Road, Nottingham, at Hucknall Road, and the vehicle was going to Oxton on route 8.

Above: In 1939 the Leyland Lion models delivered were again to an upgraded version: the LT8; there were dual-purpose 39-seaters from both Duple and Brush. Number **336** (**EVO 32**) was the second of the Duple examples. It is seen at Barton's headquarters at Chilwell in August 1948. This vehicle was later fitted with a Leyland 8.6-litre diesel engine and lasted in the fleet until 1954.

Below: Another of the same batch of LT8 Lions, No. **342** (**EVO 38**), was fitted with a similar engine in 1950, as well as the Duple body formerly carried by No. 264, a 1936 LT7. In this Mount Street, Nottingham, view of July 1950, the Leyland Tiger radiator that came with the new engine is evident.

Above: A new member of the Leyland menagerie appeared in the Barton fleet in 1939/40 in the shape of a batch of 14 Cheetah LZ4 models, all with Brush 39-seat dual-purpose coachwork. Number **360** (**FNN 671**) is seen at Mount Street in January 1947; it was withdrawn the following year.

Below: New buses were not easy to come by during the war and although many second-hand vehicles - mainly double-deckers - were acquired, the first new deliveries were in 1942. They included a Leyland Tiger TS11, No. **424** (**FVO 325**), fitted with a Willowbrook austerity 36-seat front-entrance service bus body. It is on the right of the pair in this picture at Mount Street in January 1947. The other vehicle is No. **261** (**BVO 461**), one of the 1936 LT7 Lions, which had been rebodied with a similar body, but by Burlingham, in 1944. Both were to receive postwar bodies.

Above: The wartime Tiger TS11, No. **424 (FVO 325)**, is seen here after rebodying in 1948. The Duple 35-seat coach body had come from No. 484, a 1947 Leyland Tiger PS1/1, which was rebodied as a dual-purpose 39-seater, again by Duple. This is an August 1949 Mount Street view.

Below: Postwar rebodying of the prewar Leyland Lion chassis was not uncommon. Here, No. **253 (BVO 453)**, a 1936 LT7, which had been rebodied with a Burlingham austerity body in 1944, is seen with the 39-seat Duple coach body that replaced the Burlingham unit in 1949. Another 1949 Mount Street picture, this time in June.

Above: The early postwar period was notable for the continuation of the Leyland/Duple partnership for new Barton vehicles. PS1/1 Tiger coaches started appearing in the fleet in 1946 and continued in some numbers until 1949. This example, No. **489 (HVO 125)**, was a 1947 delivery, photographed at Mount Street in August of that year.

Below: Duple had all of Barton's orders for new coachwork at this time, but 1947 Tiger PS1/1 No. **490 (HVO 729)** carried a body built by the operator. American influence showed in the small windows with their horizontally sliding vents. An October 1955 photograph.

Above: The side profile of the Duple design was one of the most attractive to be seen. This Barton example, regrettably unidentified, was bathed in spring sunshine at Mount Street in May 1949.

Below: Exactly a year earlier, at Melton Mowbray, this photograph was taken of one of Barton's 1947 Bedford OBs. Number **525** (**JAL 30**) had a Duple 27-seat body and was one of eight delivered during the year. In 1950 this vehicle was fitted with a Chevrolet engine; in 1951 it was reseated to 20 and then in 1954 to 24; it was withdrawn later in 1954 and went on to run for Atkins and Daly, trading as Premier Coaches, of Nottingham.

Above: LT7 Lion No. 319 (**DRR 975**) of 1937 was in 1950 fitted with a Leyland 8.6-litre oil engine then in 1953 received the 1948 Duple 35-seat coach body formerly carried by Leyland PS1/1 Tiger No. 538. It was also renumbered as **538** when the latter was withdrawn for rebuilding as a Barton BTS1 (No. 716). The new No. 538, seen above at Mount Street in March 1954, was withdrawn in 1958.

Below: A similarly complicated story attaches to No. 311 (**DNN 239**), which in 1954 received a 7.4-litre Leyland diesel engine, with in this case a postwar Tiger radiator, and a Duple body from another postwar PS1/1 Tiger No. 544, and was renumbered **544**, as seen in this March 1956 picture.

Above: Barton's reputation for experimentation and flamboyance suffered not all in 1950 when, among the Bedford OBs and the BTS1s that were just coming into the fleet, this Leyland CPO1 Comet appeared. The fully fronted 32-seat coach body was by Beccols. The Comet model was to semi-forward control specification: this one had been converted to forward control by Barton. Number **620** (**LAL 849**), seen here when brand new in June 1950, was withdrawn in 1963.

Below: An equally unusual vehicle in the same year was No. **621** (**LNN 968**), a Churchill-bodied 34-seat coach on the Commer Avenger chassis, also seen when new, operating on a tour to North Wales. It was outside Barton's office in Huntingdon Street, Nottingham.

Above: The single-deck fleet in the early postwar years was, as we have seen, largely a Leyland/Duple affair - both new chassis and rebodied prewar - with a small contribution from Bedford. As the new decade started, two new strands developed: the Barton BTS1s and an intake of second-hand vehicles. The BTS programme involved constructing chassis from withdrawn prewar Leyland Titan double-deckers: No. **597 (NNN 81)**, for example, had a front end from Wigan Corporation TD4 No. 91 and the rear from Bolton No. 87, a TD3c. The coachwork, to dual-purpose 43-seat standards, was built in Barton's own workshops. It was photographed at Mount Street in May 1953.

Below: A number of Tigers and Titan double-deckers were bought from the West Riding Automobile Co Ltd, of Wakefield, in 1949/50, including No. **602 (HL 9074)**, a Roe-bodied Tiger TS8 32-seat service bus dating from 1939. In August 1950, very soon after its repaint into Barton colours, it was photographed at Mount Street.

Above: Apart from the Leyland Comet sold to Barton in 1950, Leyland Motors placed a Tiger PS2/3, which became No. **630** (**LNN 886**). It had fully fronted 43-seat dual-purpose coachwork by Beccols and was spotted by the photographer at Huntingdon Street when brand new in August 1950. The PS2/3 chassis was designed for 27ft 6ins bodywork, whereas this Beccols 43-seater was 30ft-long, and Barton's own workshops did the conversion work to alter the chassis.

Below: Identical coachwork from Beccols graced the first Barton BTS1 *(see picture and caption on page 2)*, seen here at Huntingdon Street on a misty day in November 1951.

Above: Barton BTS1 No. **633** (**MAL 389**) had coachwork to Barton design built by Strachans as a 41-seater. The components for this vehicle came from two prewar Burnley, Colne and Nelson Leyland TD3c Titans: No. 88 donated the front end and No. 94 the rear. Number 633 was withdrawn in October 1963 but not scrapped until 1968.

Below: Number **633**, and identical sister vehicle No. 635, were rebuilt, resulting in a less bulbous outline. Both these pictures were taken at Mount Street, the first when the vehicle was new and the second after the rebuild, in November 1955.

Above: Number **634** (**LVO 560**) was another example of Barton's rebuilding to make use of running units from two Burnley, Colne and Nelson TD3c Titans: Nos 92 and 98. The coachwork, to Barton's Viewmaster design, was the first for the BTS1s to be built by Barton staff. Photographed in February 1952, LVO 560 was a September 1963 withdrawal.

Below: Scenes like this were a commonplace at Chilwell during the BTS1 building programme. The yard was full of second-hand prewar Leyland Titans waiting to donate their running units to new BTS1s. Identifiable are ex-Wigan Corporation Nos **87** and **88**, which donated their front ends to Barton Nos 659 and 656. The photograph was taken in September 1950.

Above: In the midst of the BTS1 programme, the underfloor-engine revolution caught up with Barton. In 1951 a batch of five Leyland Royal Tigers with Burlingham centre-entrance 39-seat coach bodies was delivered, epitomised by No. **674 (MRR 154)**, seen at Nottingham Broad Marsh in January 1952, acting as a Barton Enquiry Office. All five were withdrawn in 1954 and were sold to Heaps Tours, of Leeds.

Below: The rather heavily engineered Royal Tiger was replaced by the lighter Tiger Cub, and Barton took five Alexander-bodied examples in 1954. One of them, No. **677 (RAL 799)**, was at Drummond Road, Skegness, in July 1954. The Tiger Cubs had rather longer lives with Barton than had the Royal Tigers, not being withdrawn until 1973.

Above: Meanwhile, the BTS1 programme continued into its later stages, when the donor vehicles changed from prewar bought-in Leyland Titans to Barton's own single-deck chassis. Among them was No. **709 (PNN 107)**, which was Leyland Lion LT5a No. 182, dating from 1934, lengthened and fitted with a Leyland 8.6-litre diesel engine and the Duple 39-seat coach body, lengthened to 30ft, from Barton No. 542, a Leyland PS1/1 of 1948. The new combination retained its original radiator and was perhaps the most unusual of the BTS1 conversions.

Below: Another variation on the theme was to commission new coachwork from Plaxton for BTS1 rebuilds, typified by No. **711 (OAL 714)**. This one gained its chassis from Barton PS1/1 No. 536. In this May 1953 photograph it was carrying an all-cream livery.

Above: Alongside the programmes of rebuilt BTS1s and new underfloor-engined single-deckers, as almost always in the Barton story, there was an intake of second-hand vehicles from acquired operators. Such transactions brought all sorts of miscellaneous vehicles into the fleet, often bearing little resemblance to Barton's direct purchases, as in the case of No. **680** (**FCT 943**), a 1951 Bedford SB fitted with Brush 33-seat coachwork, acquired from J Randall, of Asfordby, in August 1953. Barton replaced its petrol engine with a Perkins P6 diesel unit later in 1953 and used the vehicle until 1955.

Below: In September 1955 a large part of the fleet of Allen's, of Mountsorrel, was acquired. It included **BJU 366**, a 1939 Daimler COG5/40 with Willowbrook 39-seat coachwork, which became Barton No. **757**. The eight ex-Allen vehicles (four Daimlers and four Leylands) were withdrawn between 1957 and 1967; No. 757 went in 1959. The Daimler double-decker behind was No. **755** (**CUT 857**), a 1945 Brush-bodied Daimler CWA6, which was the first ex-Allen vehicle to be withdrawn, in 1955.

Above: Representing the Leylands from the former Allen fleet is Barton No. **760 (FUT 7)**, a 1949 Willowbrook-bodied 34-seat Leyland Tiger PS1/1. Photographed in May 1956 in Rick Street off Huntingdon Street, Nottingham, it was withdrawn in 1958.

Below: The underfloor-engined section of the fleet was augmented in 1955 by the first AEC Reliances. The first was No. **740 (SNN 773)**, new in the April, the month of this photograph at Mount Street. The 45-seat dual-purpose coachwork was by Alexander. The vehicle lasted 19 years and was withdrawn in 1974.

Above: Plaxton coachwork also appeared on AEC Reliances in 1955: examples with 38, 41 and 45 seats being specified. Number **742 (SRR 620)** was a dual-purpose 45-seater, which was withdrawn in 1973. It was photographed in July 1955, the month after its arrival in the fleet. It is shown here as a 41-seat coach but was altered very quickly to a dual-purpose 45-seater.

Below: The AEC underfloor-engined chassis must have given satisfaction for a number were sought via the second-hand market. Number **750 (RTA 228)** was a year old when bought in 1955 from Rambler Coaches (S J Wakley), of Axminster. The centre-entrance 41-seat coachwork was by Strachans. This is a July 1958 photograph and the vehicle was withdrawn in 1972.

Above: Another second-hand centre-entrance 41-seater on the AEC Reliance chassis, also bought in 1955, was No. **751 (135 BMV)**, acquired from C E Parlane Ltd, of Aldershot. The coachwork was by Duple and the vehicle had originally been an AEC demonstrator: hence the Middlesex registration. This one also lasted in Barton service into 1972.

Below: Another 1955 addition to the fleet, No. **752 (XRB 33)**, was a 41-seat coach of a very different specification. A Commer Avenger II, it had Duple coachwork, was acquired from Lindley's Garage Ltd, of Long Eaton and withdrawn in 1961.

Above: Second-hand Duple-bodied AEC Reliances continued to trickle into the fleet, including a pair of 1955 43-seaters in 1957 from Creamline Motor Services, of Bordon. Number **772** (**NOR 511**) is seen in July 1957 at Huntingdon Street, Nottingham, immediately after its repaint into Barton colours. In pursuit was a fine Wolseley 6/80 saloon. The vehicle was withdrawn in October 1969 and its chassis used in Barton rebuild No. 1130 (YRR 508H).

Below: In 1958 the operation was repeated when a pair of the previous year's Duple-bodied AEC Reliances came from Creamline. Geoffrey Atkins was even prompter off the mark with this picture of No. **801** (**RHO 905**) in September 1958, for although it has Barton fleetname and fleet-number transfers, it is still in Creamline livery. A similar fate befell this vehicle: withdrawn in September 1969, it contributed its chassis to Barton rebuild No. 1132 (YRR 510H).

Above: Nineteen-fifty-nine saw a remarkable variety of single-deckers added to the fleet, starting with a batch of six Alexander-bodied AEC Reliance front-entrance 41-seat coaches, one of which was No. **813 (813 CAL)**, seen in August of that year. It lasted for 15 years, becoming transport for a jazz band in 1974.

Below: With consecutive fleet and registration numbers, No. **814 (814 CAL)** was a very different animal. A Ford 570E front-engined chassis with Plaxton 41-seat coachwork, it lasted only until 1961. It was photographed at Llandudno in August 1959 when just two months old.

Above: The Ford 570E chassis also appeared in the Barton fleet in 1959 with Duple 41-seat coachwork. Number **815 (815 CNN)** is seen in February 1960 at Huntingdon Street awaiting its departure time for a service journey to Leicester. The vehicle lasted five years longer than No. 814, being withdrawn in 1966.

Below: To further confuse the onlooker in 1959, similar Duple 41-seat coachwork appeared on the Bedford SB1 chassis as Barton No. **821 (821 CVO)**, photographed in Huntingdon Street in August 1959 on its way to Skegness. It was withdrawn in 1970.

Above: A single AEC Reliance with coachwork by Thomas Harrington, of Hove, also came in 1959. The 41-seater is seen in this view at Llandudno in August 1959. Number **825 (70 DNN)** was a 1971 withdrawal.

Below: Amid the variety of 1959's new coaches, surely the most bizarre was No. **826 (467 DRR)**, a 12-seat Morris J2BM minibus bought for use on airport transfer work for Barton's own services. The number and destination box in the front dome was fitted by Barton. Four years were enough, and it went in 1963. In this picture it was at Broad Street, Nottingham, in April 1960.

Above: Nineteen-sixty saw further coachwork variety on the Beford SB1 chassis. Number **829** (**829 ENN**) was bodied by Burlingham to the usual 41-seat forward-entrance specification for this chassis. In another shot of a brand new vehicle, it was at Mount Street in June 1960. It was withdrawn in 1971.

Below: It was becoming quite a habit to buy pairs of almost new AEC Reliances from other operators, and in 1961 Barton bought Duple-bodied 250 MML and **280 SMG** from Empire's Best, of North London. The latter is seen as Barton No. **860** at Granby Street, Nottingham, in July 1961.

Upper: Yeates, of Loughborough, and Plaxton, of Scarborough, also built bodies on the Bedford SB1 chassis for Barton in 1960. One of the Plaxton examples, No. **872 (872 HAL)**, was photographed at Stamford in March 1961, with a Duple-bodied Leyland Titan behind.

Centre: Plaxton was again the coachbuilder in 1961 for a batch of seven AEC Reliance 41-seaters. In a scene at Derby bus station in August 1967, No. **863 (863 HAL)** was working the express service X34 to Llandudno. The vehicle was withdrawn in 1974 and found further work with an independent operator in Wales.

Lower: As late as 1961 Barton acquired examples of the wartime Bedford OWB model, when a pair came with the acquired fleet of Cream Bus Service, of Stamford. Number **881 (ATL 238)** had been rebodied in 1952 with a Duple Vista 29-seat body. Although withdrawn by Barton later in 1961, ATL 238 was used: it was not, however, repainted and in this view in the yard at Chilwell it had a "BARTON" sticker in the windscreen. Alongside was No. **555 (KAL 152)**, a 1948 Leyland Tiger PS1/1.

Upper: The Bedford SB1 was proving to be quite a useful vehicle and more came later in 1961 with bodywork by Duple or Burlingham. Number **908 (662 KNN)** was one of the Duple versions, a 41-seater, seen here at Huntingdon Street in September 1965. The combination of a frontal profile usually associated with private hire and excursion work and destination and route number boxes for stage carriage work was very characteristic of Barton. Number 908 was withdrawn in 1971.

Centre and lower: There were three Burlingham-bodied Bedford SB1s in 1961, including No. **911 (283 KVO)**, seen in the centre view in July 1964, with a destination screen incorporated into the front bumber bar and the word "ENGLAND" at the top of the radiator grille. In the second view, taken in May 1965, the dome had been substantially rebuilt to include a route number box and "ENGLAND" had disappeared. Number 911 also lasted a decade and was withdrawn in 1971.

Upper: As the sixties moved on second-hand AEC Reliances continued to find favour and yet another former unit of the Creamline, of Bordon, fleet appeared with Barton. Again Duple-bodied, as a 43-seater, No. **905** (**VOT 678**) had been new in June 1959 and moved to Barton in March 1961. As late as 1969, when this picture was taken, it was looking immaculate, despite which it was withdrawn in 1971.

Centre: Number **914** was a similar Reliance/Duple, purchased in July 1961. Registered **VHO 500** in April 1959, it was recorded as having come from Parlane's (Aldershot) Ltd, of Bordon, but had been licensed to Creamline. It had not yet been repainted in Barton livery in this August 1961 view at Huntingdon Street. The vehicle was withdrawn after being badly damaged by fire and its body scrapped. The chassis was rebuilt and used for BTS2 No. 1204 (HVO 473K).

Lower: An important acquisition in October 1961 was the fleet and business of Robin Hood (Coaches) Ltd, of Nottingham. The oldest of 19 vehicles taken over was **KNN 749**, a 1949 AEC Regal III with a 1954 Duple Vega body, which became Barton No. **921**. It was at Huntingdon Street in August 1964 and was withdrawn later that year.

Upper: The ex-Robin Hood additions to the fleet included three 37-seat Weymann Fanfare-bodied AEC Reliances, which dated from April/May 1955. In this April 1963 view one of them, No. **928 (SNN 509)**, still had the raised aluminium "Robin Hood" fleetname as well as the Barton flag. SNN 509 worked for Barton until 1969 when it was withdrawn, its body scrapped and its chassis used in Barton rebuild No. 1136 (YRR 514H).

Centre: Ex-Robin Hood **239 CNN**, Barton No. **933**, was a Duple-bodied 41-seat AEC Reliance that had been new in April 1959. Upon withdrawal in 1971 it was sold to Invicta Bridge Engineering, of Newark. The photograph was taken in August 1969.

Lower: The Robin Hood vehicles taken over comprised 15 AECs, three Leylands and a solitary Bedford: a C5Z1 model with 29-seat Duple coachwork. Registered **149 FVO** and dating from May 1960, it became Barton No. **935** and survived into 1971; it was then sold to a new owner in Northumberland.

Upper: Coachwork from the Hove factory of Thomas Harrington was not common in the Barton fleet at this time. From Robin Hood came four 1960/1 AEC Reliances with 41-seat bodies from that coachbuilder, including No. **936** (**99 GAL**). All four were withdrawn in 1974 and this one went to the Welsh independent Llynfi Motor Services, of Maesteg.

Centre and lower: Always at the forefront of vehicle maximisation, Barton nonetheless caused something of a sensation in 1962 with a batch of six dual-doorway Yeates-bodied 36ft-long AEC Reliances, more especially with three of them that had no fewer than 57 seats. Numbers **947/6** (**947/6 MRR**) are shown when still quite new with a livery designed round the Yeates body embellishments. Number 946 had 49-seats; 947 was a 57-seater when new, later altered to 49. All six were eventually converted to single front-entrance 51- or 53-seat (947) coaches.

Above: The Yeates maximum-capacity exercise was repeated in 1963, this time using the six-wheeled Bedford VAL14 chassis. A batch of seven included four 50-seat coaches and three dual-purpose 56-seaters: all seven had two doors for separate passenger entry and exit. Number **963** (**963 RVO**) was the first of the batch and one of the 50-seaters. It is seen leaving Nottingham for Loughborough, followed by a Ford Consul saloon and a Nottingham City Transport AEC Regent.

Below: Number **968** (**968 RVO**) was one of the 56-seaters, seen here at a futuristic-looking Mount Street bus station in November 1970. Both these VAL14s were withdrawn in 1973.

Above: In 1961 there were also four VAL14s with Plaxton 52-seat coachwork, all of which were withdrawn in 1973. In this September 1971 Mount Street scene two of them are featured: No. **970** (**414 SRR**) and No. **972** (**650 SVO**) demonstrate the provision and lack of sliding vents to the side windows.

Below: The VAL14 story continued into 1964 with examples bodied by Harrington and Duple. Representing a batch of eight Harrington examples is No. **992** (**992 VRR**), seen in Huntingdon Street, outside the bus station, in September 1968. The Harrington VALs were withdrawn in 1970 (991) and 1973.

Above: There was a distinct air of anticipation in the early sixties as Barton's fleet numbering crept towards 1000. It was thought likely that that milestone would appear sometime in late 1964 and, in the demonstration park at the 1964 Commercial Motor Show at Earls Court, so it did: No. **1000** (**ANN 700B**), another VAL14, bodied by Duple. This view at Derby bus station was taken in August 1966 and the vehicle was withdrawn in 1973

Below: Three Bedford SB5s with Duple Northern Firefly 41-seat coachwork were further 1964 entrants into the fleet. Number **997** (**997 XNN**) is seen in August 1969. It was a 1973 withdrawal.

Above: Among all the Bedfords, which were regarded within the industry as "lightweight" chassis, Barton in the 1960s still favoured the "heavyweight" concept for a proportion of its fleet. In 1964/5 this resulted in two batches, of ten in each year, of magnificent Harrington-bodied 51-seat AEC Reliance coaches. From the 1964 deliveries is illustrated No. **980 (980 VRR)**, seen loading at platform eight in Huntingdon Street bus station for a run to Blackpool on the express X61 in June 1964. The vehicle had been new earlier that month.

Below: Number **1005 (BVO 5C)** from the 1965 batch displays an example of those detailed differences among similar vehicles that made the Barton fleet so fascinating. The destination screens were set into the grille on the front panels, in place of the Barton fleetname, instead of in the roof dome. This meant the loss of the AEC badge, for the fleetname had to be moved up into its position just below the windscreen. The vehicle was brand new in this July 1965 picture, in the same place and on the same service, having been delivered earlier that month.

Above: The lightweights entering Barton service alongside the AEC Reliances included in 1965 a batch of 15 Bedford SB5s with Harrington 41-seat coachwork. Number **1012 (BVO 12C)** features in another picture of a brand new vehicle, and was at Huntingdon Street in August 1965.

Below: A pair of rather different Bedford SB5s was acquired, second-hand from Price, of Romsley, in January 1965. The Yeates coachwork, extended beyond the front axle, allowed 43 seats instead of the normal 41 for an SB. The first of the pair was No. **1026 (508 GUY)**, photographed in July 1965, and it was withdrawn in 1971. The other, No. 1027 (509 GUY), went a year later.

Above: From the sublime (the AEC Reliances) to the ridiculous in 1965, when two Bedford CALZ30s with Martin Walter 11-seat coachwork arrived. A use was found for them for four years and in 1969 both found new owners. Number **1028** (**DNN 647C**) was the first of them, seen nestling among some of its full-sized brethren at Huntingdon Street in August 1967.

Below: An example of what today would be called a midibus also added to the variety in 1965. Number **1030** (**EAL 557C**) was a Bedford VAS1 29-seater, bodied by Duple. It lasted until 1973. It had ventured as far as Llandudno in this July 1966 picture.

Above and centre: The next year - 1966 - was also a good one for AEC Reliances. Another batch of ten 51-seaters was bought, this time with coachwork from Plaxton. Fine as that coachbuilder's products were, perhaps these vehicles had not quite the majestic air imparted by the two earlier batches bodied by Harrington. Number **1063** (**FVO 63D**) is seen in August 1966 at the top of King Edward Street, Nottingham, on its way to Blackpool; No. **1069** (**FVO 69D**) was at Llandudno a month earlier.

Lower: Eight Reliances were among the twelve vehicles acquired from Provincial Garage (Leicester) Ltd in May 1966. Plaxton-bodied 49-seater No. **1058** (**45 DJF**), new in 1962, was, if the destination blind in this picture can be believed, on a Scottish tour as late as 1973.

Above: The value for money in being able to carry 45 passengers on a lightweight chassis ensured continuing sales for the Bedford *marque*, and in 1966 Barton took eleven VAM5s - ten with Plaxton bodies and one from Duple. One of the Plaxton examples, No. **1072 (FVO 72D)**, is seen at Huntingdon Street in August 1966, neatly framed by Nos **768** and **774 (URR 868** and **YNN 774)**, 1956/8 AEC Reliances with Plaxton and Alexander coachwork respectively.

Below: The solitary Duple-bodied Bedford VAM5 in 1966 was No. **1082 (JNN 128D)**. This vehicle entered service in an all-over cream livery; by the time of this July 1967 view at Huntingdon Street, it had gained Barton colours.

Above: AEC Reliances were bought new as long as they were available, and in 1967 yet another batch of ten - again with Plaxton coachwork, this time seating 53 - was purchased. In the parking area at Huntingdon Street bus station in April 1971 was No. **1100 (LVO 100E)**, the last of the batch. It was withdrawn in 1974, as were all the others save No. 1095, which went a year earlier.

Below: In August 1971 at the same spot - in the intervening four months the scaffolded building behind No. 1100 in the picture above had been completed and the tree had burst into leaf - stands No. **1129 (FUP 272C)**, a 1965 AEC Reliance with Willowbrook coachwork. This had been purchased in August 1969 via a dealer, and had been in the fleet of Stanhope Motor Services Ltd, of Frosterley.

Above: October 1971, and the tree is leafless again. Barton's No. **1122 (BCU 282C)** was a Duple-bodied Bedford VAL14 52-seater, which had been new in July 1965 to Hall Brothers (South Shields) Ltd. Barton purchased the Hall Brothers operation in July 1967 but for a short period it was maintained as a wholly owned subsidiary. Gradually the vehicles were given Barton fleet numbers and livery and merged into the main fleet.

Below: There was a strong echo of Barton's early postwar rebuilding programme, which created the BTS1 vehicles, when in 1969/70 ten Barton BTS2s were produced. Major differences, however, were that, whereas the BTS1s had been based on Leylands, the BTS2s were constructed from rebuilt AEC Reliance chassis; and that all the coachwork was ordered from a single outside supplier - Plaxton. Representing the batch 1130-9, at Loughborough in February 1970, is No. **1131 (YRR 509H)**, which was based on the chassis of No. 778 (MHO 362), a 1954 Reliance acquired from Barry's Coaches, of Moreton-in-Marsh in 1958.

Above: A further batch of ten new AEC Reliances with Plaxton 53-seat bodies appeared in 1970/1. One of them, No. **1144 (OAL 769J)**, was photographed at Mount Street in November 1970 alongside two earlier examples of the breed. Duple-bodied 41-seaters Nos **932/3 (229** and **239 CNN)**, dating from 1959, had come from Robin Hood Coaches in 1961.

Below: Before their final absorption into the main fleet, the ex-Hall Brothers vehicles were to be seen with fleet numbers in an "H" series. Part of the fleet was transferred in 1969 and the remainder in 1971 when the Tyneside - Midlands services were transferred to Barton. In this March 1970 picture, 1966 AEC Reliance **DCU 146D** had the fleet number **H25**. It would later become No. 1172 and be withdrawn in 1974.

Above: Hall Brothers, as we have seen, were Bedford and AEC users; they also had a number of Leyland Leopards: one was **ECU 759E**, which became Barton No. **1178**. By then looking very "Barton", the vehicle was photographed in January 1974, the year of its withdrawal.

Below: As the 1970s got under way, Barton's vehicle policy underwent a dramatic change. The previous mixture of new, acquired, in-house-built and second-hand stock was to be replaced by a vast fleet of Leyland Leopards and Bedford YRQ and YRT models and there were to be no more double-deckers. Among the earliest YRQs was No. **1187 (GAL 20J)**, a 1971 example from a batch of eleven with Willowbrook 52-seat dual-purpose bodywork. Possibly written down deliberately over a short working life, they had in any event all gone by the end of 1976.

Upper: In the absence of the AEC Reliance, no longer available following the merger of AEC and Leyland, the Leyland Leopard was to be the heavyweight representative in the new fleet policy. Number **1191** (**GAL 24J**) of 1971 was one of four in that year. Their Plaxton bodies had 53 seats. All four were withdrawn in 1976 and none outlasted any of the year's lightweight Bedfords.

Centre: The Bedford YRQ with Plaxton coach body seating 45 is shown in a view, at Mount Street in February 1972, of the previous year's No. **1201** (**HVO 470K**).

Lower: Duple was to have a considerable share of the coachbuilding as Barton's replacement new vehicle programme took on momentum in the 1970s. Here is a 1973 Bedford YRT 53-seat coach, No. **1325** (**WRR 363M**).

As the seventies progressed the Barton fleet took on more and more of a sleek, streamlined look, containing as it did nothing other than single-deckers with Plaxton or Duple coachwork that all looked the same: but then - did the enthusiast of 40 years earlier, used to the amazing Barton variety of the twenties and early thirties, think that the Leyland Lions all looked the same? It is at this point that we take our leave of the single-deck fleet, as seen through the cameras of Geoffrey Atkins across a period of around sixty years, by contrasting Nottingham street scenes of the thirties and the late eighties. In the January 1989 picture *(above)* at Long Row is No. **533** (**ERB 533T**), a 1979 Leyland Leopard Plaxton 53-seater. The fleet numbers, although in the same sequence, had now dropped the "1". In the background, overtaking ex-London Transport Routemaster **314 CLT**, owned by K & M Gagg, of Bunny, is No. **617** (**A617 ATV**), a Plaxton-bodied DAF and a pointer to the next generation. The appearance of operators other than Nottingham City Transport in the Old Market Square, which included Long Row, was a post-deregulation phenomenon. Below is No. **154** (**VO 7405**), a 1932 Leyland Lion LT5 35-seater (also bodied by Leyland), passing a Nottingham tram as it heads out towards Derby. In the misty background is a Midland General Tilling-Stevens. The tram is on the London Road, Lenton and Radford route 7: this was changed from "7" to "F" on 5th March 1933, so the Lion was in its first months of Barton service.